Have the happiest of birthdays,
and a year filled with adventure,
friendship and love.

To: Gill

From: Cathy

with love

26ᵗᵉ

October

1996

May you never cease to find new
possibilities in life
and in yourself.
May you hold a quietness inside
yourself that nothing
can destroy.
May this year be exactly the way
you'd like it to be.

A birthday to remember

I wish you a world where you can find your way, and love your work and find great happiness. I wish you a birthday to remember with a smile. And years of discovery and joy.

I hope the road leads you
through sunlit countryside.
May no river be too deep to wade,
no rock be too difficult to climb.
Adventures. Surprises.
And the attainment of your
dreams – your secret hopes.
The gifts we cannot give.

What can I wish for you on your
birthday that's better than the
usual things?
Opening the curtains in the
morning and finding snow.
The first few drops of rain
printing the dust of drought.
Windows ablaze with sunset.

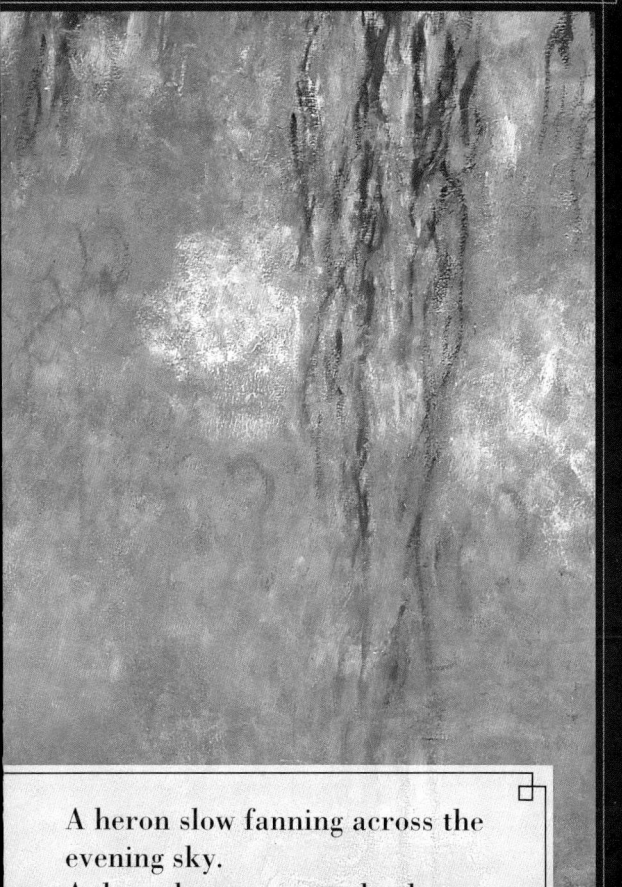

A heron slow fanning across the evening sky.
A door that opens on the dear familiar things.
The smell of spring.
Things you already have.
But always new.
The gift of days. The gift of life.

I wish you great joy on your birthday.
I wish you astonishments, laughter, song and talk and hugs and kisses.
May every day to come hold good surprises, unexpected joys.
May your every wish come true!

May all your plants grow strong
and true
– whether a flower or a fruit, or
an idea –
A book, a cabinet, a family, an
engine.
A song!

Birthdays have a way of
falling on days cluttered with
ordinary events
– but I wish you flowers
and cards and packages
and hugs bobbing up between
the dull things, all day
long.

This is a day for remembering.
For smiling over funny, happy,
silly things.
For sighing over sadnesses.
But it is a day for celebration,
too, and a looking-forward
to new wonders, new
astonishments, new joys.

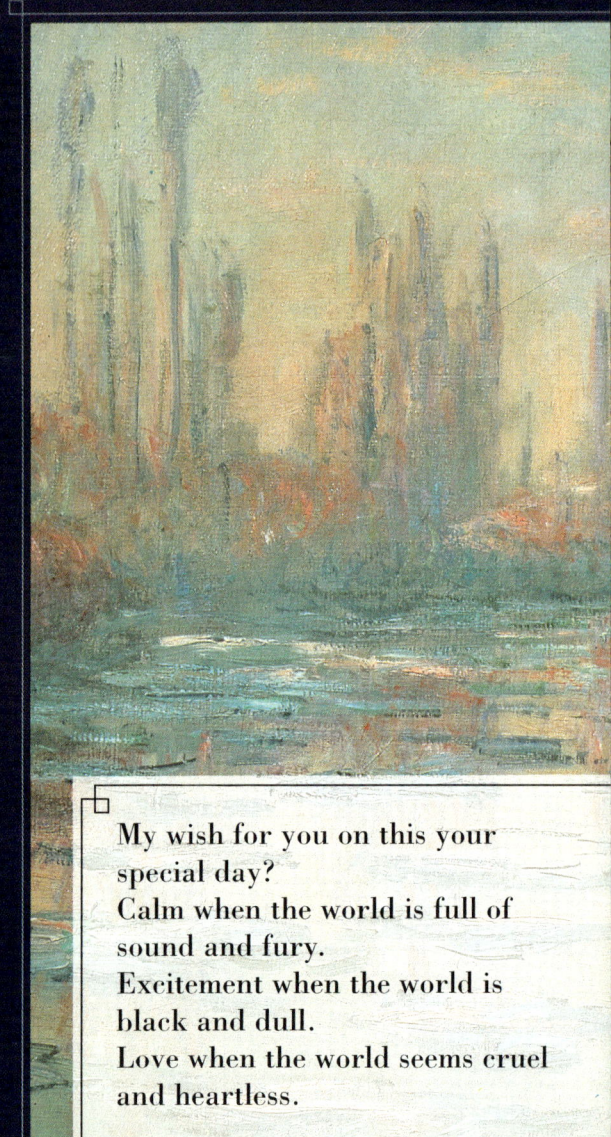

My wish for you on this your
special day?
Calm when the world is full of
sound and fury.
Excitement when the world is
black and dull.
Love when the world seems cruel
and heartless.

Everyone in the world is important.
But today you are especially important.
May the day be as wonderful as you deserve.
Let the coming year be even better.

The true gifts

I wish you star-studded skies,
a blackbird singing to
the dawn, diamond-bright
spider webs, rainbows in the
grass and the slow, sweet
spreading of light.

If the world were a sensible place
everyone would be given the
day off on their birthday – and
a bottle of champagne and
tickets for an adventure and a
splendid meal.
Ah, well. – A happy, happy day
all the same!